BOYS

BOYS

ANONYMOUS

ISBN: 978-93-5614-105-6

Published: -

LECTOR HOUSE LLP
E-MAIL: lectorpublishing@gmail.com

BOYS:
THEIR WORK AND INFLUENCE

Tenth Edition.

CONTENTS

INTRODUCTION.

The following papers were written at the request of one who had read the somewhat similar papers addressed to girls. The object aimed at in both books has been to try and help Boys and Girls of the so-called working classes to recognize their duties to God and their neighbour, and to use on the side of right the powers and opportunities which God has given them.

It seems to the author that advice given to the so-called lower orders, often partakes too much of patronage, and too little of the brotherhood, that should be a sign of Christians. "Do as you are told and be thankful," is too much the tone of the advice, instead of explaining duties, pointing out opportunities, and recognizing them as fellow-labourers in the great work.

In God's household everyone has his place assigned to him by the master, some to govern, and some to serve, but still all are fellow-servants of that one Master, and brethren in Christ.

BOYS.

What a curious fellow a boy is. I wonder if boys ever think about themselves. A young monkey is full of mischief, a young puppy is full of play, a young kitten is always ready for fun, but a boy seems to combine the qualities of all three, and to have a stock of his own to jumble up with them. A boy has so many sides, not only an outside and an inside; he is a many sided being. See him at one time and you would hardly suppose him to be the same creature that you had seen a little while before. Now he is a bright nice spoken lad, in a few moments he is a bullying tyrant, now he is courteously answering those who speak to him, now words come from his lips that shock the hearer. Now he would scorn to have his word doubted by a comrade, now he does not hesitate to lie to escape punishment. Now fearless, now a coward, now full of spirits, now in the depths of woe—sunshine or joy, wind and calm, silence and tumult, all seem to have their place, and to make up that incomprehensible and yet delightful animal a boy.

Now boys, I want you to think of yourselves—not to think how good or how bad you are—what fine fellows you are, and what important persons, but what you are capable of becoming. You will not remain boys always—you are now, in the midst of all your oddities, forming your character, and shaping your future course, drawing out of the midst of all your contradictions the character that will make you honest God-fearing men, like in your degree to the perfect pattern of manhood which God has set before us in Christ—or you are letting yourselves be moulded into the selfish sensual being, which too often degrades the name of man.

Thinking, I know, is not much in your line at present, but you will perhaps spare me a few minutes, and give me a little of your attention while I try to point out to you the way in which you may, if you will, turn your powers to account, and avoid the dangers which have been the shipwreck of many a lad's bright prospects.

HOME AND SCHOOL.

I shall take it for granted that you care for your parents and home, or at any rate that you would like to have a comfortable home. Well, then, make it so yourself. You can do a great deal towards it. Honour and obedience is your first duty towards your parents. There is nothing manly in disobedience. Honour and obey, readily and cheerfully. Not simply obedient to father because he might thrash you; and disobedient to mother because she cannot compel you. No, the truest honour in a boy is when mother can thoroughly trust him—trust him to obey her because she is mother.

Brothers and sisters are often a trouble. "How those children do nag?" "Never can leave those boys together." "He's sure to teaze her if I leave them alone." Don't be a bully either to your brothers or sisters. Don't be selfish and claim all you can for yourself. Share and share alike should be the rule, and gentleness towards the girls and little ones.

School will help to take the nonsense out of you; you cannot have it all your own way there. Boys will be boys, is a very common expression, and it would be very funny indeed if boys did not turn out to be boys, but that is no reason that boys should be rude or cruel, and in fact "little cubs." Quarrels there will be sometimes—very often for no real reason, sometimes for a good cause. If you have one fight it out then and there, and bear no malice afterwards. I would rather see a fair fight and have done with it, than keeping up a nasty quarrel, and trying to spite one another in little mean ways. There is too often a want of real honour amongst boys. Telling tales of one another seems to be the fashion, and the favourite way of paying off old scores. There are of course times when a boy must speak out against wrong, even at the risk of being counted a sneak, but, as a rule, boys who delight in telling tales, and who have not the sense of honour to stick by one another are a very poor lot.

Do your school work thoroughly. Idleness is not only wrong but foolish. There is a time for work and a time for play. Learn as much as you can and learn thoroughly if you want to be of any use in after life. A boy's religion is not a thing that shows very much on the surface, or that he is very likely to talk much about, but it must be in him if he is any worth.

Boys and girls alike should learn from their mother to say their prayers night and morning, and when they become too old, or mother too busy for them to say them at her knee, they should never omit to say them by themselves. I heard the other day of a rough labouring man, who on his death bed sent for the priest of his parish. He said he had never been inside a Church since he had been a man.

He had done his work honestly, and lived steadily, but had altogether got out of the way of going to Church. There was one thing, however, that he had always done. Long years ago, as a lad, he had promised his mother never to get up in the morning or go to bed at night without saying his prayers. This promise he had kept faithfully. Night and morning that rough strong man had knelt and said the same prayers which he had first learnt at his mother's knees. Those prayers had been heard and had brought their blessing to him. Church going on Sunday is as important as daily prayers. A Sunday morning should never be allowed to pass without seeing you at Church. Lie a bed on Sunday morning is the devil's version of the fourth commandment. There is plenty of time on Sunday for Church as well as for walks and talks. Sunday is not to be a miserable day, or all Church and prayers, but God first and then ourselves. Sunday school you will most likely be sent to as long as you go to day school, and you will be wise not to give it up as soon as you are what you would call your own master.

Both home and school ought to have their pleasures as well as their work. Do your work thoroughly, and do your pleasures thoroughly also. Share your pleasures with the others, and with father and mother. You can give much pleasure to father and mother, as well as to yourselves, if you try.

Love God and love your home—be obedient, truthful, and plucky—standing up for the right, and not ashamed to refuse to join in the wrong; and your home and school days will train you well for your work in life.

GOING TO WORK.

What are you going to be? is a question that has to be settled very early in life—earlier amongst the so-called working classes than any other. It must be settled at about thirteen years old. Fortunately for you it is not whether you shall do anything for your living or not, but in what way you shall earn your living. Some people seem to look upon work as if it were a degrading thing, and only to be used until they can afford to live without it. Life is not worth calling life that is not downright honest work, and a man is hardly a man at all who is not a working man—working either with his hands or his brain, or both.

In determining what your calling in life shall be you must consider two things, 1st. Whether the calling you wish to follow is an honest and lawful one. 2nd. Whether you are fitted for it.

If you can say yes to both these questions, then, provided your parents approve, follow out your natural inclination. A lad is far more likely to succeed in life if his heart is in his work, than if he has to work against the grain. On the other hand, you will never deserve success if you go against your parents' wishes. If they see reasons against the particular calling you wish for, (and perhaps are really fitted for), your duty is to follow their wishes, and bide your time. If your inclinations really point to that to which God calls you, He will show you the right way to it in His time, and your obedience to your parents will not have been wasted time.

There are certain occupations which are not honourable, but by which men gain a living, which are not to be considered for a moment, as *e.g.*, gambling and betting. There are certain for which you would not be fitted by education or ability. Whatever calling you choose seek God and His righteousness first, *i.e.*, choose that which will make you fit for the next world as well as that which will make you comfortable here. Honest work thoroughly done here will be no bad passport for another world. When you have once chosen your calling stick to it, carry it out thoroughly, and with a determination to get on. Never be in a hurry to change, and never do so without a good reason. Never rest satisfied that you have done enough, or think that you cannot do better. It is told of a celebrated sculptor, that he said, "I shall fail in my next effort, for I am satisfied with this."

Aim high and do your best. Every shop-boy may not become a Lord Mayor, but every one who aims at getting to the top of the tree, and goes steadily at it, will find himself at last a good way from the ground.

Now supposing you have made your choice and started in work you will find a great difference between this and school life. You will mix with elder people and a different set; you will have more freedom, and possibly a little more money.

Don't think you are a man all at once, because you are nothing of the sort, and nothing makes a lad look more ridiculous than to see him trying to be a man before his time. You know the story of the toad and the ox.

You have much to learn yet. Stick to classes and learn all that you can. Sunday classes as well as night classes. There is nothing manly in giving up religious duties; quite the contrary, it is cowardly. Do your work honestly and thoroughly, even though it be the custom to do otherwise. Boys are pretty sure to have some hobby of their own, and a very good thing too. A boy is all the better for a hobby, even if he takes it up and drops it again. It is a good thing for a lad to have some private interest of his own. If therefore your hobby is not anything harmful follow it out with a will.

RELIGION.

I had some doubts about the heading of this chapter: Religion ought not to be a separate thing from daily life, and, therefore, all remarks on the subject ought to come under one or other of the chapters which treat of the different duties of life. There are, however, certain definite religious duties which may perhaps be spoken of more clearly in a separate chapter. I would ask you always to bear in mind that no religious duties are of much value that are not a regular part of our daily life, and that there is no line to be drawn between natural and religious duties. "Whether, therefore, ye eat or drink, or whatsoever ye do, do all to the Glory of God."

Prayer, private and public. What I have said in a former paper holds good now. No boy can safely neglect his morning and evening prayers and his public worship on Sundays. Prayer should include daily self-examination: no one can get on in the world unless he looks after his own affairs, and reckons from time to time how he stands. So with our daily life—we should try it day by day, and see if we are keeping straight. Each night we should look back over the day, see what has been wrong, what imperfect—seek pardon for the wrong, and determine, by God's help, to amend it.

Public Worship once a Sunday, *i.e.* in the morning, is the duty of every Christian: whether we go oftener is a matter of choice, but less we cannot do without failing in our duty. Attendance at the full morning service, *i.e.* the celebration of the Holy Communion, is the prayer-book rule, whether we observe it or not.

Regular Communion is absolutely necessary. How frequently it is advisable to come must depend upon circumstances, but speaking generally I should say, in the words of one whose opinion carries great weight, that "monthly Communions are the very fewest which anyone seeking to serve God devoutly can make."

I have taken it for granted that you have been confirmed, which will probably have taken place about the time of leaving school. Confirmation ought to make a marked change in your life. Firstly, because you are more directly responsible for yourself, and, secondly, because it brings you into closer relation, for a time at least, with your clergyman. Before your first communion the prayer book speaks to you very distinctly about personal advice and intercourse with your parish priest. Neither your first or any subsequent communions are to be made unless you are satisfied as to your own fitness to come to it. If you are in doubt you are advised to go to God's minister, lay before him those sins that make you afraid or doubtful of coming, and seek his advice. This is not pleasant, but it is useful. Many people speak against it, but it is Christ's appointed way. If you feel that this will help you, go as often as you need, and do not be stopped by any foolish remarks of people who do not understand it, or by any thought of its being a weak and unmanly thing to do. It requires courage, perseverance, and a true estimate of oneself to do it, and these are not generally considered unmanly qualities. Some of the best men, some of the bravest soldiers, have not been ashamed of using this means of grace. Knights of old were accustomed to confess before they went into battle. Read the life of Henry V. of England. He was no milksop, or, as people would say now-a-days, priest-ridden king, but he did not look upon it as an unmanly thing. You are free to choose, or free to refuse it; only pray to be guided aright by God's Holy Spirit to do that which shall be most to His glory and your soul's good.

Almsgiving. Whatever money you have of your own some portion—a tenth, if possible,—should be given to God in some way or other.

Bringing others to God. We must not be selfish in our religion—if God has made known the truth to us we must do our best that others may share it also. You can do much in a quiet way, not only by example: you can get a word in where others have not a chance. Many a youngster would gladly keep from wrong, and go on steadily, if he had only someone to stand by him. It is not enough to be good, we must do good, and never laugh at another for his religion. Many years ago a thorough change was worked in a school by the courage of one little boy. He came fresh from home, where he had been accustomed to say his prayers. He knelt down in a school dormitory, as he had been used to do at home, by his bedside. There was a sudden silence, the boys were astonished. Then some began to bully and try and stop him; others stood up for him. But the battle was won. The better minded boys saw what cowards they had been to give up what they knew was right for fear of chaff—one by one they gradually followed his example, and before that lad left school it was the rule and not the exception for the boys to say their prayers.

Fasting. People understand feasts and are ready enough to keep them, but fasting is quite another matter. Feasts should be kept, and the more the great festivals are recognized the better. Fasting, however, is quite as necessary. Appointed times in which to remember more particularly Christ's suffering for us, to deny ourselves lawful pleasures, and to make us think more of our sins and how to conquer them. They keep us from getting careless, and letting our religion become a sort of Sunday clothes, to be put on at certain times, but to have no real effect upon our daily life.

One thing more. God has given you brains and the power to use them. You are bound then to try and learn about God, and the duty you owe to Him. Every year you ought to advance in knowledge, and not be content with the little you were taught as a child. Read your Bible—think it out for yourself—pray for understanding, and study such books as will help you to a better knowledge of it.

COURAGE.

Boys and men are great cowards. There is hardly any accusation that an Englishman or boy resents so much as to be called a coward. Still I venture to make the accusation, and will try and make good my words. I do not mean that you are cowards in the sense of being afraid to attempt any act of daring. You have pluck enough to tackle a fellow half as big again as yourself, pluck enough to endure pain without a word, pluck enough to risk your life to save another, but too often you have not pluck enough to say no, or to brave a laugh. That is what I mean by saying that men and boys are cowards. You will let the worst fellow of the lot be the leader and give the tone to conversation because you have not the pluck to say boldly that it is wrong, and that you will not join in it. This want of moral courage makes a lad give up little by little his hold on what is right. Sunday school, Church-going, prayers given up because Jem chaffs so about them. If he chooses to neglect them that is his look out. You have as much right to your opinion as he has to his. Why should you let him show more courage in doing wrong than you in doing right. Are you afraid of him? No. Well then, stick to your duty.

I said just now that going to work throws you in with a different set of companions. Here, specially, comes the test of your courage. Are you going to follow bad leaders, or have you the courage of your own opinions. There is one particular subject where courage is most needed, and where it most often fails. A young lad naturally wants to seem to be manly—has a sort of feeling that he would like to show that he is not just a little boy and bound to do as he is told. He is tempted to show his manliness by neglect of home commands, rough and rude manners, bad language and bad talk. I have remarked before how home obedience and true manliness go together; here I want to speak more particularly about bad language and bad talking, and the evil it leads to. S. Paul speaks about it very plainly when he says, speaking of the things that should not be named amongst Christians, "neither filthiness nor foolish talking nor jesting, which are not convenient." Now, boys, all indecent words and conversations are wrong—they are sinful, unmanly, degrading. I know you cannot help hearing much that is wrong. Shame, be it said, to the men of England—yes, men who talk of advancement and freedom, men who are fathers of families, that they too often make or allow the talk of the workshop to be such that no boy can work there without hearing words and jokes which are not fit, I do not say for Christians to hear, but not fit to be spoken. Hearing words of evil you often cannot help. To join in them you can and must refuse, and unless you do so refuse you are a coward and false to your profession. I do not speak here of actual deeds of sin—no one can do or join in an impure deed without knowing that he is sinning, but many think that there is no great harm in listening to and laughing at what others say. Be warned in time, it is but a very little step from laughing at to joining in bad conversation, and a very small step from words to action. The same want of courage that joins in the laugh will make it difficult to say no when tempted further. Never, with companions of your own sex, and still more with those of the opposite sex, let any corrupt communications proceed out of your mouth. If it is necessary for you to speak upon such subjects ask advice of those older than yourself, and not of companions of your own age. You know lads that you love your mother and care for your sisters. You would be furious if anyone spoke to or of them as you sometimes hear women spoken of. What would be an insult to them is an insult to any woman. Stand up for the honour and respect due to others as you would for your own mother or sister. You would not talk like that before your mother. Make it a rule never to do or say anything that you would be ashamed to say in her presence, or in the presence of anyone you respect. Courage is what you want here and plenty of it, but if you will only make a stand for the right, strength, not your own, will be given you. I can tell you of one who did so try and do the same. Bishop Pattison, who died some years ago, when he was fearlessly doing his duty in the islands of the Pacific, was, once a boy, face to face with this difficulty. He was in the cricket eleven of his school—a good player and very fond of the game. It had become the custom at cricket suppers for bad talk to be indulged in. Pattison one evening rose up at the table and said, "If this conversation is to be allowed I must leave the eleven. I cannot share in this conversation—if you determine to continue it I shall have no choice but to go." They did not want to lose him, and the foul conversation was stopped.

MONEY.

The love of money is the root of all evil. Nevertheless, money in a civilized country is a necessity. How to make it is one of the great questions, and how to spend it aright is one of the great difficulties.

Money is power. It is power, if we use it aright, it overpowers us if we use it badly or even carelessly. It is a great mistake to want to make your money too quickly, and a still greater mistake to think that you are likely to do so. Money that is the result of honest labour will, if rightly used, be a blessing to you and yours.

1st. How to make it. By honest labour, honestly done. You have chosen your trade or occupation—let your money be honestly earned therein, and look more to the quality of your work than to the quantity of your money. You have a right when you have learnt your trade to a fair day's wage for a fair day's work, but be sure that the word fair governs both the work and the wage—the fair work must be done before the fair wage can be rightly claimed. There is far too much scamping work in the present day, working simply for money and not for any interest in the work itself. Money should not be a man's test of success, but the perfectness of his work. Men used once to work for love of their art, and so long as the picture was painted or the sculpture wrought, they cared little for the money they were to gain by it, or the hardship of their lives, but now men paint for what the public will pay for, and write and work not from their hearts but for their pockets. And with high and low, not success but money is the moving power—not how can I can make it more perfect, but what can I get for it. A man who will leave a piece of work, or a clerk who will leave a few minutes writing only because the clock has struck the hour, is little better than a money-making machine. Work done in such a spirit did not give us men like Wren or Stephenson. Read their lives and you will see what I mean. If your work is thoroughly and honestly done, you have a right to your own price for it, if you can find a purchaser. You have a right to sell your labour at your own price, but the master has an equal right to buy or to refuse. Combinations and unions of working men are perfectly right, if they unite for their own advantage, and for protection against oppression, and strikes may, though in very rare cases, be a painful necessity. It must be borne in mind that there can be no fixed standard of wages. Wages must vary with the state of the markets. Men must be ready to accept lower wages when trade is dull, they must bear their share of the depression as well as the masters, and the true principle is for men and masters, or if you like the expression better, capital and labour to go hand in hand. The success or ruin of the one is the success or ruin of the other. There are of course cases of grasping masters who will endeavour to grind their workmen, and there are cases of worthless and obstinate workmen, who look only to themselves and the present moment, but both ought to be and might be very rare exceptions, if the good and true men on both sides would come to the front.

2nd. How to spend the money. Remember that you are God's steward, and will have to account for the use of this bounty. Give your tithe to God first. The tenth part of your profits, whether reckoned weekly or yearly, should be given to God in some way or other, and those who do it will find themselves blessed in earthly things, whilst they are laying up a treasure in heaven. God's tithe paid, how is the rest of your income to be spent? 1st. Necessary expenses, *i.e.*, food, clothing, &c. 2nd. Useful expenditure, *i.e.*, learning, books, &c. 3rd. Recreation and minor luxuries.

Pay your way as you go, and never run into debt. Debt is next door neighbour to theft. Two things I would impress upon you, first, that where the need is you should repay your parents care by helping them. England is disgraced by the number of old people who are left to the care of the parish by children who ought to be thankful to be allowed to support them. Secondly, that it is your duty to make provision for the future, so that the workhouse may not even enter into your calculations, as a possible refuge in old age for you and yours. This can be done by regular savings, even though very small, and by insuring your life. Post office and other savings' banks, will help you in the former, and various insurance offices offer special facilities by weekly and monthly payments for the latter.

AMUSEMENTS.

Recreation is as necessary as work. What kind is to be sought after, and what avoided? For health's sake, if for nothing else, boys should have some kind of out-door amusements. A boy has an easy choice of good and healthy recreation, and therefore has no excuse for taking up with bad objects. Cricket, Rowing, Volunteering, and such-like, are healthy, and easily obtainable recreations. Gambling, drinking, loitering, are not to be thought of for a moment, they are the curse of the lazy and weak-minded. Theatres are very good if you keep out of the cheap and nasty ones. Music halls are much better avoided. I do not say that it is necessarily wrong to go there, or that you are certain to come to harm if you frequent them, but there is more chance of temptation, and an inferior entertainment for your money. Well acted plays may open out your mind, but the silliness of the music hall entertainment will only react upon you. You can tell a music hall frequenter, not by the words of his mouth so much as by the shuffle of his feet: his highest ambition seems to be to dance the double shuffle, and perhaps sing a few verses of some jingling rhyme. Out-door recreation is not so easily attainable, in the winter, as the time at your disposal is so short. In-door amusements must, to a great extent, take their place. The gymnasium is a good institution; chess is a game worth learning, and very fascinating to some minds; cards are good as long as gambling is avoided, and many other games readily suggest themselves to one's mind.

Reading will be more to the liking of many. Read books which are worth reading, not the penny trash which shops offer to the boys of England. I should hope that the boys of England have sufficient brains to care for something a little above the penny dreadfuls, otherwise it is a bad look out for the future men of England. Independently of libraries you can now get books, by good writers, as cheap as sixpence—Walter Scott, Fennimore Cooper, Maryatt, Dickens, &c. A word about books. Of course, in books by writers such as I have mentioned you will find many things spoken of which are wrong and ought not to be. They must write so if stories are to be written of life as we find it, and mere goody-goody books, which avoid all mention of such things, are unnatural, and do not give true pictures of life. The harm of too many cheap publications, and not only the cheap ones, is, that in speaking of these things they make them appear unavoidable, and even worthy of praise. Good writers show how revolting crime and evil is, how they can be overcome and resisted, and how truth and honesty must prevail in the end. The difference between good books and plays and bad ones is not so much the subjects they write about as the way in which they speak of them. Some of the cheap literature is only foolish, some is distinctly wicked, but both are better avoided, and your time and money spent on worthier objects. Avoid bad company, and take care that your recreations are manly and honest.

HOME DUTIES.

As soon as you begin to bear your share in the expenses of home, you will naturally look to have your word in the arrangements thereof. From the time that you begin to earn your own living, until the time that you make a home for yourself, there will be certain home duties which you have no right to neglect.

First of all, you must be ready to bear your fair share in the expenses of the home. When first you go to work, you will probably be expected to bring home all your money, and have a certain sum given to you for pocket money. As you grow older, you will agree to pay a certain sum for your board and lodging, and keep the rest for yourself. Let your payments be such as will do a little more than actually cover the expense of what you have. Give a thought to the general comfort of the home, and in time of need when perhaps your father's work is slack, be ready to increase your help, even though it may decrease your own personal comfort.

Secondly, you must acknowledge the authority of the head of the house, and respect his wishes as to home arrangements, time for being in at night, &c.

Thirdly. Recognise your responsibilities to your brothers and sisters. If you are the eldest son you are bound to be the example, and if need be the protector of the others, and whether elder or not you have still your duties and responsibilities. A good brother is a great help to a sister, and her brother's good opinion will be something which she will be very sorry to forfeit through any fault of hers. For your sisters' sake specially you are bound to be careful that your companions whom you may bring home with you should not be such as would not be fit company for them. Your duties to your parents I have already mentioned, and the older you grow the more thoroughly you should carry them out, so that, as you grow out of mere boyhood, you may become more and more the companion and friend of your father, and more and more the comfort and support of your mother. It is a great thing in time of trouble to have one son to whom they can look without fear of his help failing them. It is far too common to see young fellows, so soon as they can earn enough to support themselves, leaving home and going into lodgings because they are freer and more comfortable, and leaving their parents to struggle on with the youngsters. It is a selfish and ungrateful course, and therefore sure to be without a blessing from God. I am talking now of those whose work keeps them near home, and who only leave their home to escape its duties, or as they would miscall them, its burdens. Many, of course, must leave home. If work calls you elsewhere it is another matter. It would be a very good thing in many instances if young fellows would have the pluck to emigrate and make their way in a new country. Englishmen are getting too fond of stopping at home where the labour markets are overstocked. Emigration is one of the best openings for a young fellow if he makes up his mind to work, and does not expect a fortune to fall into his lap because he has gone to a new country to seek it.

SELF-IMPROVEMENT.

Boys generally leave school at about thirteen years of age, but they make a very great mistake if they leave off learning at that age. Time might be roughly divided off into four parts—necessary work, work for others, self-improvement, and recreation. A man's education is never completed. A man is never too old to learn. Whilst you are a boy and lad you need to be taught; afterwards you can to a great extent learn for yourself. You should never be content to remain just where you are, you should endeavour to make the most of your opportunities, and to advance in knowledge and capability. You are taught in your catechism to "do your duty in that state of life unto which it shall please God to call you." This does not mean that you are not to try and better your position. Quite the contrary; it means that while you are to go on contentedly in the station and work which God has allotted to you, you are also to try and use to the utmost all the opportunities and powers which he has given. He has called you to your present position, He may be calling you to something more. If he has given you the power and opportunity of raising yourself, he meant you to use them. It is a false humility and a false view of religion that encourages sloth under the pretence of being contented with one's humble lot. There is God's work—real every day work to be done in worldly as well as in what seems to be more directly spiritual work. One's whole interest is not to be centred on earthly things, neither are we to be so heavenly minded as to neglect earthly duties, and the talents which God has committed to our trust. It is your duty then to do your utmost to improve your stock of knowledge. School has laid the foundation, and you must work at the building. Your own particular tastes or your work will suggest the subjects to which you should first turn your attention. Develop the natural powers you have, and advance steadily from one subject to another. Set apart a certain portion of your spare time for study and self-improvement. Remember also that you have certain duties to your neighbours and your country, and that in order to fulfil them you must understand your position as a man and a citizen. Read the history both of your own country and of other lands. Read your paper. Study the questions of the day, both at home and abroad, and learn to form your own opinion concerning them. Learn to think for yourself, and not take as gospel all that you read in your favourite paper. Look at both sides of a question and make up your own mind. Comparatively few people think for themselves, and for that reason men are so often carried away by popular leaders, and obstinately follow opinions, the truth of which they have never tested, and the consequences of which they have never considered. There are many opportunities in classes and lectures for men to gain information, but they will be of little real use unless men will think for themselves, and work out the subjects instead of taking their opinions ready made. Study, not simply listen. Study both secular and religious subjects. You may be sure that there can be no advance in real self-improvement unless it is well balanced. Religious knowledge should go hand in hand with secular knowledge. Christ should be our great example in this as in all else, and He "increased in wisdom and stature, and in favour with God and men."

CHUMS.

Birds of a feather flock together. A man is known by his friends. It is of great importance therefore that your friends should be such as will show that you yourself are of the right sort. A boy, unless he is a particularly disagreeable one, will probably have a fair number of friends, that is to say, of fellows that he knows and associates with, but above and beyond these he will probably have some one particular chum, one who shares in all his plans, one with whom to talk over all his schemes, one often with whom to join in some piece of mischief. Chums to do one another much good should be about the same age. There may be a friendship between an elder and a younger boy, or between a boy and a man, but they will not be exactly chums. A friendship of this sort is very useful if the elder is one who will lead aright, but if the elder is the weaker of the two, or still more if the elder is viciously inclined, such an acquaintance is one of the worst possible things for a lad. A young boy, hanging on to an elder one, learning all his bad habits, is only too likely to prove an apt pupil, and come utterly to grief. Remember no one is worthy of the name of friend who would ever counsel you to do anything wrong, or who would not give you a word in season when he found you were going on a wrong tack. A chum of one's own age is quite a different article. Very often they are not lads of the same dispositions and tastes, and are drawn to one another by these very differences. It not unfrequently happens that a bright active lad will chum with a very quiet meditative one. The one doing the thinking and the other the acting. Such friendships will last on sometimes through life, but generally well through boyhood. Very often the last act of chumship is the acting as best man at the friend's wedding. Such friendships will work great good so long as they are on the give and take principle, and that nothing is given or taken of the bad qualities which may be in each. A boy without a chum is very likely to grow either conceited or selfish, or both. A good-natured chum is a very useful check. He does not mind chaffing him out of any little absurdities, and rubbing against one another they manage to knock off many odd corners and polish up one another. Any chumship in evil is to be avoided. If a chum, however much he may be liked, wants you to go in for a partnership in evil he must be given up. I don't say that you can give up caring for him, but he must be made to see clearly that he must make his choice between the evil doing and you—that he cannot be chums with both. Chums should have strict honour between themselves, and always be ready to stand up for one another. A good chum prevents one becoming a prig, and there is nothing short of actual vice which is so hateful in a boy as priggishness. There is as much difference between a prig and a right-minded boy as between chalk and cheese. A right-minded boy goes on his way trying to do right and live honestly and purely, because it is right and honourable, and because deep in his own heart he knows he has promised Jesus Christ that he will live a godly life. A prig is also doing right and living purely and honestly, but is all the time trying to make other people see it, and not doing it simply because it is right. Hence he has not half the strength when real temptation comes, because he has always been looking at the outside effect of his life, instead of looking inward, to see if he is true to his promise. Avoid priggishness, but do not be afraid of being called a prig when it is only the taunt by which someone hopes to shame you into doing that which you know in your heart is wrong.

COURTSHIP.

There comes a time when a young man begins seriously to look forward to settling in life and having a home of his own. As a boy he may have had his likings among the girl companions with whom he was acquainted, but now it becomes a totally different question, and his intercourse with young women assumes the position of courtship.

It is only natural and right that man should look where God intended him to look for a help-meet and companion, but all depends upon the way in which he does it. There is no need to be in a hurry. Better to wait and make quite sure. As a general rule I should say that twenty-five was quite young enough for a man to marry, but still that must entirely depend upon circumstances.

Before I venture to suggest a few thoughts concerning courtship and the choice of a wife, I should like to make a few remarks upon the manner in which women ought to be treated by men. It is too much the custom for men to look upon women as beings the object of whose creation was to be pleasant companions for them before marriage and useful servants after marriage. Hence there is a very great want of respect and honourable treatment. A young fellow, before he steadies down as the expression is, does not think there is anything mean or dishonourable in his leading a girl on, and without any intention of ruining her, allowing her to lower herself by her conversation and manners. He does not consider the harm that he is doing to the girl, how it may be the first step to ruin. He means no harm, only just amusing himself with her. Is it not mean, however, simply for his own pleasure to treat a woman as if she were merely a plaything, instead of a being as valuable in God's sight as himself, and equally with him an object of God's love and care. No words suffice to denounce the wickedness and meanness of the coward, who, taking advantage of a girl's real though misguided love for him, will seduce her into sin and then leave her to bear the punishment and disgrace. No words can describe the heartless wickedness which will rob a woman of that which is her greatest treasure and ornament, and bring upon her a sorrow which the grave alone can end. He may escape punishment here. He may even gain a sort of reputation as one who can always gain the attention of women, but he will only receive the greater punishment from the judge and avenger of all. One word more before I close these remarks, which I would have gladly omitted from these papers, but truth demands them.

Some men seem to think that the sin and responsibility is very slight if it be committed with a woman who trades upon her sin. Undoubtedly it is not so cowardly as the ruin of a pure and innocent woman, but who can tell that you may not have met with that woman at the turning point in her life, when but for you she might have repented? and at the very least you have added to the weight of her sin. Once she had been pure, God alone knows her history, but who of the many who have taken advantage of her misery and helped to chain her to her life of sin will be held guiltless by Him? Great, fearful is her guilt, but God alone knows how she may long to be free. Far greater is their guilt who for their own selfish enjoyment do not hesitate to plunge deeper into ruin a soul for whom Christ died. If men treated all women honourably—all, not simply their relations and friends,—there would not be those who make their living by sin. Such a state of things it may be hopeless to expect, so long as cowards are to be found amongst men, but it is not too much to expect from honourable men and Christians that they should treat all women with such respect, that, as far as lies in their power, the stigma of meanness and cowardice should not rest upon the men of this land. Treat them with respect, not only in your intercourse with them, but in your conversation about them, and your thoughts concerning them.

But to turn to a pleasanter subject, the honourable courtship of man and maiden. Certain things should be taken into consideration in making your choice. First, that the object of your choice should be one whom you can thoroughly love and entirely trust. Secondly, that she should be one whom you feel would be a real help in life. Thirdly, that she should be of the same religion as yourself (otherwise difficulties in after life are sure to arise) and a really religious woman. And Fourthly, that she should be not merely, or even necessarily, a bright and pretty companion, but should have such qualities as are necessary for a good wife and mother—one who can manage a home as well as help to pass an hour or so pleasantly.

Your courtship should be thoroughly open and above-board. The parents consent should first be obtained, and remember that you are bound to respect their wishes. Be careful also that she shall never in any way be compromised by your conduct. I say no more because I have assumed at the beginning that your courtship is honourable, that you love the girl of your choice, and that as you would shield her from all injury from others, so she will be safe under your protection. Take no ordinary standard as the rule of your courtship, but determine from the very beginning that it shall be so conducted, that when as man and wife you look back upon it, it may be with feelings free from any taint of sorrow or shame; that when you stand before God to be married it may be as honest man and maiden, seeking for God's full blessing upon your married life, as it has rested upon your unmarried days. One thing I would say in conclusion, and I mention it last as being the most important, let your choice of a wife be a subject of earnest prayer to God, and when your choice has been made, and your love pledged one to another, let it be a subject of mutual prayer that each may help the other to live to the glory of God, in the station of life in which he sees fit to place you.

HUSBANDS.

The headship of a family carries with it heavy responsibilities. We may shrink from them and avoid them, but still they remain. A good husband and a good father makes a happy home and honest children. Drunkenness is too often the destruction of home. If the head of the family can rule himself in this as in other matters then he may reasonably hope for a happy and comfortable home, but if drink is allowed to take the place of wife or children, drink will rule the household and swallow up its peace and prosperity. Nevertheless, drunkenness is not by any means the only fault or indeed the beginning of the break up of a home. It is very often the result of a home made miserable by other and easily avoided faults. Many I suppose start their married life with the full intention of realising their ideas of a happy home. The picture is very pleasant, the reality is too often quite the reverse. Why? Very often because of a want of mutual forbearance. It takes some little time really to know one another, and unless there is a spirit of mutual forbearance the little differences will become great quarrels. The husband is to rule, but he is not to be a tyrant. The wife is not bound to give a blind obedience to all his commands, and the husband is bound to respect his wife's wishes. It ought to be a rule that in matters of importance, where either feels it to be a question of duty, that if they cannot agree neither should endeavour to force the other to act against their conscience.

My first piece of practical advice to husbands would be to have a proper understanding about money matters, and to be liberal therein. Give your wife a regular sum per week, and let it be clearly arranged what expenses she is responsible for.

Secondly, do not have any friends that you cannot or do not care to bring to your home, and let no one come between you and your wife, or draw you away to enjoy yourself apart from her.

Thirdly, do your church-going together as far as you can, and when that is impossible arrange one with the other, so that each may be able to go at some time every Sunday. Above all keep one another up to your regular Communions, for there is little blessing on the married union that is not blessed with a higher communion.

Fourthly. When you have children train them yourself, specially the boys, who will gain far more good from father than from anyone else. It is too much the custom to leave all the religious training to mother or to school. Take your children to Church with you instead of seeing that they are sent. Come is a much better word of instruction than go.

A few words in conclusion as to the general duties of a man, be he married or single. You have no right to shirk your duties as a man to your home, as a Christian to your Church, or as a citizen to your country. The support and training of your family is your first duty, and nothing may rightly come in the way of that, but the fulfilling of that need not prevent your carrying out your other duties. You are a Christian, you receive spiritual benefits from your connection with the Church, you are bound then to make some return. Your prayers, your alms, and your active work, according to your means and opportunities, ought to be available for the work of the Church. There ought not to be any drones in the Church's hive, but each member should bear his share of the burdens, as well as partake of the blessings. There is work for everyone that is ready to help.

You have still your duty to your country. Your own personal influence may not be great, but you are nevertheless bound to use it on the side which you believe to be right. Public opinion is made up by the agreement of many, and the course of the nation is guided eventually by the votes of the people. You have your share in the responsibility of all that is done, and are therefore bound to endeavour to understand the questions of the day, and to act upon the conclusions you may form. No man has a right to shirk any of the responsibilities of his position, and a true man will endeavour to serve God and his fellow-men to the best of his ability—to do as much good as he can in the little time allotted to him, and to leave the reward of his labours in the hands of Him for whose sake and after whose example he has endeavoured to spend his life.

Lector House believes that a society develops through a two-fold approach of continuous learning and adaptation, which is derived from the study of classic literary works spread across the historic timeline of literature records. Therefore, we aim at reviving, repairing and redeveloping all those inaccessible or damaged but historically as well as culturally important literature across subjects so that the future generations may have an opportunity to study and learn from past works to embark upon a journey of creating a better future.

This book is a result of an effort made by Lector House towards making a contribution to the preservation and repair of original ancient works which might hold historical significance to the approach of continuous learning across subjects.

HAPPY READING & LEARNING!

LECTOR HOUSE LLP
E-MAIL: lectorpublishing@gmail.com